Breaking the Cycle of Lust

Dwight K. Buckner, Jr.

Breaking The Cycle of Lust
Are you ready to be free from sexual sin?

Dwight K. Buckner Jr.

Book cover/design by Dwight K. Buckner, Jr.

Cover Art by Daniel Ojedokun (Danny Media)

Published and distributed by Dwight K. Buckner, Jr.

Edited by Constance Nicole

ISBN: 978-0-578-62797-7

Produced and published December 2019

Tucker, Georgia, United States of America

This book is dedicated to my wife, Elisa J. Buckner, for believing in me and constantly encouraging me to write about something so personal. I would also like to dedicate this book to my best friend, Andre Sifford, who serves as our executive pastor at the Generation of Hope Church. He said to me, "Pastor, Breaking the Cycle of Lust will be your first book." Thank you both for your support and love.

I also want to thank God for using me to advance His kingdom. He and He alone gets the Glory!

Pastor Dwight Kevin Buckner, Jr.

INTRODUCTION

Life is filled with cycles. A cycle is defined as a series of events that are regularly repeated in the same order. Your life is filled with cycles. You might have had a cycle of different jobs that you worked and each job may have focused on the same thing. You might have had a cycle of back pains that just will not go away. You might even have had a cycle of bad relationships and you are wondering, "God, why me? Why does this keep happening?"

Cycles can be good or they can be bad. In this book, I will attempt to explore the cycles of negativity that have been lingering over our lives. Months back, I did a series entitled "Cycle Breakers." In this series, we explored the many cycles we sometimes face in life.

Until this series, I had no clue exactly how many negative cycles we deal with—such as cycles of depression, cycles of poverty, cycles of suicide, cycles of anger, of bitterness. Did I hit yours yet? There are cycles of lying and cycles of stress. The list goes on and on. However, there is good news. The good news is that these negative cycles can be broken. These cycles can be broken!

Cycles and curses are closely connected. A generational curse is basically a defilement that was passed down from one generation to another. This is what you call a cycle of curses. Let's just get into it!

All families have different cycles of curses that they deal with—drinking, smoking, fornicating, etc.

However, I am willing to bet that most of us—most of us dealing with these curses that have been handed down—most of us did not choose these negative cycles. Many of us were born into dysfunction. We did not have a choice. We were born into this world with boxing gloves on, fighting against these cycles that we did not choose and certainly do not deserve.

For instance, a young lady might be born into a family where her mother and father were drug users. Growing up, she may have witnessed her parents using drugs in the home, on the regular. From the outside looking in someone else would see it and recognize it as a negative cycle, as a curse. The young lady, however, may not recognize it as a curse until she gets older because it was normal for her. She didn't know anything different. She did not know any better.

Remember Beloved, what's normal for you, may not be normal for someone else. Don't ever take the blessings on your life for granted. There is always somebody else worse off than you. My definition of a negative cycle is a repeated curse, something negative, attached to your name that you inadvertently rehearse over and over again.

For instance, if growing up I heard cursing in my home, all the time; I would unconsciously begin to repeat the same behavior. I would have grown up thinking that using profanity was normal. I may even have grown up thinking that everyone curses. I may even have wondered why others did not curse the way my family cursed. Finding out that not everybody curses may even have been embarrassing, but just because it was the norm in my family, does not make it right.

I want to be very transparent throughout this book and start by telling you that I have not been perfect by any means. I am not writing this book from the standpoint that I am some sort of expert, or as if I have a PhD in breaking cycles. I simply want to share with you a personal struggle that was a part of my life since I was a youth—that big "L" word, lust.

I have two beautiful boys, six and seven, and I have never once heard them say, "Daddy when I grow up, I want to be lustful." They have no clue what lust is at their ages. However, if as a parent, I do not share with my sons and educate them, on some level, about where daddy failed, they won't know. My sons will have no knowledge of the demons that run in the family, until it attacks them. I think God holds parents accountable especially if they know about the family curse, the cycle over the family, and they never take out time to teach their children the history of it and how to overcome it.

CONTENTS

1   The Root of Lust   Pg #1

2   Anointed and Lustful   Pg #13

3   Lust in your Family   Pg #25

4   Lustful People Hang Around Lustful People   Pg #34

5   Lust is Only in Certain Rooms   Pg #46

6   Lust Does not Care Who it Hurts   Pg #59

CHAPTER ONE—

THE ROOT OF LUST

Lust is a psychological force producing intense desire or longing for an object or a circumstance to satisfy the craving or fulfill the emotion. Lust can take any form such as the lust for sex, money, or power. It can also take more mundane forms such as the lust for food, as distinguished from the need for food.

The cycle of lust we will break before you finish this book is sexual lust. Right now, take a quick 30-second praise break and thank God that every lustful demon will be out of your body, your house, your mind, and out of your family!

EVERY FAMILY HAS CURSES AND BLESSINGS

Most families that deal with lust will tell you that someone found some of daddy's inappropriate movies, or someone discovered that momma had secret lovers—while married to daddy. In other families, someone might say that they dealt with abuse from someone within the family. I was a virgin until I was 17 years old. I did not want to sleep with anybody then, but because of the pressures of being a teenage boy, I did. I opened myself up to someone. I thought it was over, but then I started longing for another and another, and before you knew it, I had had several partners. It got to the point that I could not go to sleep without calling somebody. My mother and father divorced when I was 17, and I moved in with my mother.

Now my father, who is also a Pastor, was pretty strict. Growing up at times, I often felt like he was too hard on me. When I got older, though, I realized how much I completely appreciated him. I realized that his sternness is what kept me out of trouble.   When I moved in with my mother, I started dating and eventually, I started having sex. When I turned 18, I had already had several partners. I mean, I wanted to stop but that cycle just would not let me.

Even today, I am still amazed by the fact that I am pastoring a church—knowing my past. But before you judge me, take a second and remember where you used to be. From about the age of 18 through the age of 21, I had so many women that my mother came home one day and said, "Boy, you could be a pimp." At first, I thought what she said was cool, but only until she slid that HIV testing kit onto my bed. When I saw that, I got quiet. Eventually, I went to the doctor, often, to get checked for any sexually transmitted diseases (STDs) as well as HIV.

Thank God, I was clean, but that did not stop me. I got back into the same behavior. There was one time that I thought I caught something. I went back to the doctor and got tested for an STD—still nothing. It was like God was giving me chance after chance. Finally, I said to myself if I didn't quit, something would surface; an STD, or a child out of wedlock. To this day, I am still amazed at how God kept me! You should be too.

I began to do some research about my family, trying to figure out if anybody else dealt with lust problems. Ironically, I discovered that this cycle of lust did not start with me and it did not start with my Dad. The root started somewhere further down in the family lineage.

You see, I am a seventh-generation Pastor. That's seven strong generations of preachers. As you know, however, any time God uses a family in this capacity, especially in ministry, there has to be a great struggle somewhere. The enemy is not happy about the Kingdom work that my family has done through the years. Wherever there's great strength, there will also be great weakness. I did not ask to be born into preaching and ministry, but I was. I absolutely did not ask to struggle with lust, but I did.

THE SPIRIT OF LUST

I was born into preaching, called to preach the Word of God before I was even born. I know that God has His hand on my family. I had two cousins who were both presidents of the same seminary. Most families are proud to talk about their history. Most won't hesitate to talk about the successes or the good things accomplished by various family members, and they should.

However, what about the family members that continue the negative cycles? What about the uncle who was married five times, or the aunty that had six children by four different men? What about the cousin who sexually abused another cousin, or the brother who gets engaged to another man?

What do you say when you discover as an adult that you have three other brothers, because daddy could not keep his pants up? What would make a grown man touch and fondle a little boy? What would make a woman want another woman, or a man want another man? Why would a grown man, an uncle, touch his 14-year-old niece? Why would two teenagers experiment with touching themselves, or touching each other? How does a Pastor, a man of God, sleep with some of his staff? What would make a school teacher sleep with a student? I know. It's a spirit, and its root is lust!

What would make you get up at three o'clock in the morning and drive across town to lay in somebody else's bed? It's a spirit of lust! A man marrying another man and a woman marrying another woman is not marriage. It's legalized lust!

As believers, we have got to stop covering up family messes, and deal with it at the root. The truth is that all families have issues with which they deal. My family's issue is lust. Whatever your family issues are, you have to realize that you inherited curses, but you also inherited blessings!! Here is a quick moment of celebration for Pentecostals! Here is a shouting point! The blessing on your family is irrevocable, but the curse that's on your family can be broken!

The prerequisite is that you confront the cycle at its root, and be intentional about breaking it. I don't know about you, but I refuse to live with the demons that others chose not to cast out. If you don't get to the root of your struggle, it will forever remain with you. See, I had a seed in me that those who went before me passed down. My forefathers never addressed this seed, and as a result, I got into something lustful.

It's funny, how some family members can say negative things about you when you get into something, but they will not educate you about the root of problem. They will not talk about the curse and how it came to be—how it was passed down and came to manifest in your life. I want to set you free while you are reading this! Ask God to send you people who will be spiritual archeologists. Ask Him, "God, send me some folk who will help me discover the history of my negative cycle. Send some folk who can help me understand why I do what I do, and most of all God, send someone who will intercede for me."

LUST REQUIRES LANDSCAPING

When I was 14 years old, my father took me outside for our annual yard work, which included cutting the grass, trimming the hedges, and using the weed trimmer to get the tall grass from around the fence. Around this time, they had come out with some new spray called *Round Up*. This was strictly used to combat weeds. On the side of our driveway, we had a bed of rocks on the right, and a bed of rocks on the left. Over time, weeds would begin to grow in between the rocks, and my father bought some *Round Up*. He told me to spray all of the weeds in between the rocks. I sprayed those weeds. A few days later they died, only to reappear weeks later.

Clearly, the spray only worked temporarily. Lust works the same way. You cannot just spray lust out of your life. Trust me, it may die for a short time, but it will reappear days later. If lust is just sprayed, it will reappear in you as soon as it's triggered again. Trigger points for lust occur in your eyes and in your mind. If you visualize something sexual long enough, you will begin to desire it. You will begin to want it. If you think about it long enough, you will begin to act on those thoughts. Your actions will follow your thoughts. True deliverance is when you don't act on what you think.

Those weeds in our yard could not be sprayed away, and neither can lust. With lust, you have to go old school, like my grandmother. My grandmother had a garden for years, and occasionally we would have to work with her in her garden. I hated yard work. No matter whose yard it was, I hated it! Sorry, I am just being honest. Grandma would tell us to get down on our knees. She would tell us to get down on our knees and pull those weeds up by the root.

Eventually, we had to get down there and pull those weeds up out of the rocks, but getting down on our knees and pulling those weeds up by the root was hard work. It was a struggle, but Grandma assured us that those weeds would never grow back. Breaking the cycle of lust also requires some hard work—some knee work. You have to get down on your knees and pull the cycle of out by the root, out of the bed of rocks, which is your genealogy; so it will never grow again. You have to get on your knees and pray. You have to pull up whatever you feel will grow. I convinced that so many millennials are driven by lust because the generation that came before them did not show them how to do spiritual yard work. They failed to give them the tools necessary to pull these negative influences up by the root.

GET CONTROL OVER YOURSELF

To say that "Sex sells" is a true statement. When you see an advertisement for a new washing machine on TV with a couple kissing and taking off their clothes on top of the machine they just purchased, you are witnessing the power lust. It is absolutely absurd!

We have got to get control over our flesh. The Apostle Paul said in 1 Corinthians 9:27, "No, I strike a blow to my body and make it my slave so that after I have preached to others, I myself will not be disqualified for the prize."

In a recent commentary on this scripture, David Guzik says it like this "Bring it into subjection is literally to lead about as a slave." Paul was going to make sure that his body was the servant, and his inner man was the master. The desires of his body were not going to rule over his life. Lust was not going to rule him. When you pull lust up by the root, you are in line with what Paul said. Your body will not rule over you.

I don't know about you, but at 39 years old, I cannot afford to allow my body to make decisions for me. Some of us have too much to lose to allow our flesh to have rulership over us. Some of us need to spend time in prayer regarding this cycle. After reading this book, some of us need to ask God to pull negative cycles up out of our lives even the ones about which we have no idea. Yes, some of us have received these negative cycles from generations past and we have no idea that we are carrying on these cycles, and may even unknowingly be passing them on to our children. On another note, some of us play around too much. We know all about it. We know that we have the propensity to be lustful; the curse of lust lingers in our family tree, yet we date it, we play with it, and we toy with it, because we think it won't affect us like it did others. Yeah, okay! That is exactly how it messed up your aunt and your uncle Sam, and your great grandmother too! They too thought they could deal with it.

You better get to pulling up those roots! 2 Corinthians 10:4 says, "For the weapons of our warfare are not carnal. But mighty through God to the pulling down of strong holds." Strong holds and negative cycles in your life don't just go away. They will not leave unless you start pulling. Just think about it. If you do not deal with it, your kids will inherit the same negative cycle of curses with which you have had to deal. If you do not pull them up, you are voluntarily subjecting your seed to the same cycles of negativity; of sexual sin, abuse, excess and self-indulgence.

Now, you may be reading this and saying to yourself, "I don't struggle with sexual lust. I have overcome that." Okay! Well, the apostle Paul lists a few more things that you may not have realized fall under the umbrella of lust.

Galatians 5:19-21 says, "The acts of the flesh are obvious: sexual immorality, impurity and debauchery; idolatry and witchcraft; hatred, discord, jealousy, fits of rage, selfish ambition, dissensions, factions and envy; drunkenness, orgies, and the like. I warn you, as I did before, that those who live like this will not inherit the kingdom of God." Did you find any roots to pull up yet?

Before we get more in-depth in chapter 2, take a break and pray for God to pull the cycle of lust up by the root right now. God is ready and willing to create a fresh start with you, but you have to ask God to clean your garden from reoccurring cycles of sexual sin. Whenever a root is attached to a plant, it typically needs water and nourishment. Once it receives water and nourishment, it will extend to the other branches of the plant.

If you have always dealt with lust, chances are it spread to other branches, because of the constant attention you gave it, or the constant attention and treatment someone else gave it. Now, other branches may have to deal with lust issues including your sister, your brother, your kids, and many others with whom you deal. It is all because no one pulled it up from the root. I declare in the mighty name of Jesus that you will dig for solutions and you will not stop until you get the answers you need to conquer and break the cycle of lust!

CHAPTER 2

ANOINTED AND LUSTFUL

The word anointed means to consecrated, blessed, ordained. It also means someone that has been anointed and crowned—someone that has literally been set apart for the work of the Lord. When we see someone who is anointed, it is very clear. God makes it known that His hand is on the individual or the vessel he chooses. Sometimes the anointing can be so strong on someone's life, that we erroneously assume they are exempt from certain negative cycles, including lust.

SOME OF THE GREATEST LEADERS STRUGGLED WITH LUST

Nowadays, it seems like moral failure has become commonplace. We have become accustomed to seeing great leaders fall from grace with this cycle of lust. The church has done a good job of celebrating the anointing on the lives of great leaders, to the point that we will pardon their lust issues—as long as they can preach for us, or invite us on the platform with them so we can have our moments to shine as well.

The heart of God grieves when the church uplifts leaders who we know struggle with lust and deliberately choose not to seek help. You can be extremely anointed and also extremely lustful. I know the cycle of lust entered the church many years ago, because I started seeing what appeared to be a mass exodus from churches across the world because of this issue. I live in Atlanta Georgia and I have been in this city for over 17 years now. A few years ago. we had a very prominent leader in this city lose his ministry because of this same cycle— I'm talking about the cycle of lust.

Many in his congregation stood by him, but many more of his church members were stunned, and even ridiculed him for such acts. However, scripture tells us in Galatians 6 :1, "Brothers and sisters, if someone is caught in a sin, you who live by the spirit should restore that person gently." Many were quick to kill him with words, which makes me wonder, how many of us stopped and asked the question. Could this have been a continual cycle of lust that was handed down to him but never broken?

I am by no means minimizing anyone's pain—pain stemming from what you have gone through or what you may continue to go through. However, if the cycle is not broken, please understand that you will continue to pass it down to someone else. They will continue this same behavior; passing it down to someone else, and so on and so on. Throwing stones will only hurt temporarily, and won't solve anything. Throwing them hands up, and saying "Lord, break it!" will do so much more. Oftentimes, when we find out that someone anointed and spiritual has been caught up in sexual sin, we act shocked as if it could never have affected us like it did them. Great leaders have great responsibility, power and authority. Looking in from the outside, we really don't have a clue regarding the day-to-day temptations they may face. The Apostle Paul said in 2 Corinthians 12:7-9, "And lest I should be exalted above measure through the abundance of the revelations, there was given to me a thorn in the flesh." In his commentary on this passage in the Blue Letter Bible, David Guzik says, "The apparent purpose of this thorn was beneficiary. Its intent was to keep Paul from conceit on account of his revelatory visions."

You may be saying, *Pastor, I've had this cycle all of my life and I have prayed for the cycle of lust to be broken and it has not.* Maybe God is allowing the cycle to continue in order to keep you near Him and near the cross—not so that you can continue in your struggle. You may always struggle in this area with your own personal cross to bear. This might be God's way of keeping you on your knees before Him in prayer, *"Lord if you don't keep me from this, I am going to lose everything."*

These are not moments about which to worry. These are moments that bring you to worship and repentance. These are also moments that keep you from thinking you are the stuff. Trust me, nobody knows how to bring you to your knees like God. Paul could have said I am the man!

I wrote half of the books in the New Testament, but God made sure he remembered the continual cycle he faced. Instead of allowing him to boast in it, God used it to break him. Great Leaders have cycles with which they struggle. I mean Paul was anointed. Of that, there is no doubt, but he still struggled—he was dealing with a major cycle. Let's take a look at another of my favorite biblical characters who was anointed, but lustful. I'm talking about King David.

DAVID WAS ANOINTED AND LUSTFUL

In 1st Samuel 16, God sends for the next king of Israel. Number 1—anyone who God sends for has to be anointed. This is such a famous and familiar text that I will not bore you by repeating it here. However, David's older brothers assumed that they would be next in line for the kingship because they looked the part. Just because you look the part does not mean you can cast out devils. God was looking for someone who had his heart.

Elevation comes when God knows that your only desire is to please him. Oftentimes, I have to check my motives and reassure myself and God, that I am in ministry because He called me. It doesn't matter whether I pastor a small or a large church—as long as I am doing it for His glory and in His will. I am content knowing that He called me and that He has use for me. Jesse, David's father assumed that his older sons were more anointed than David, because they were stronger and they were already trained and skilled fighters.

That's why Samuel had to correct him, or in modern day terms, he had to check him and say "Man looks at the outward appearance, but God looks at the inwards." God looks at the heart. The Prophet Samuel tells Jesse that nobody is sitting down until you go get the son that I have not yet seen. Let me just take a moment and speak prophetically over your life and say, the world has not seen you yet. Stop coveting what other anointed people have and wishing you were like them. You want their people and their look, their style, their family, and their money. The Devil is a lie! When God made you, he broke the mold. He said there will never be another you. Be confident in your assignment and know what God has called you to do.

Verse 12 of 1 Samuel says "'So Jesse sent for him. He had a healthy complexion, attractive eyes, and a handsome appearance. The Lord said, "Go ahead, anoint him. He is the one." Samuel took the flask of olive oil and anointed David in the presence of his brothers. The Lord's Spirit came over David and stayed with him from that day on. Then Samuel left for Ramah.'"

David was not only anointed he was also

gifted. He played the lyre and he was a skilled fighter. Don't ever get your anointing confused with your gift. We have filled up pulpits around the world with just gifts. Gifted singers, gifted preachers, gifted musicians, gifted leaders, but if we are not careful, we will allow gifts to over shadow anointing. When I started the church six years ago, I could not keep any singers or musicians for anything in the world.

One year I think we went through about 20 keyboardists and 15 singers. I remember being frustrated and asking, "Lord, why are we having this problem?" The Lord had to correct me, by asking me, "Are you looking for gifted people or anointed people? Because I am only sending anointed people and that's why I keep removing the gifted ones. I was immediately convicted. I had to repent and ask God to send me people who had a heart for the ministry. I had to ask Him to send only the people who He had called to be a part of our ministry, (SEND ME THE ANOINTED ONES). God spoke over David. He said he is the anointed one. God confirmed his choice when the prophet, Samuel poured oil on David's head. God will always send another spiritual leader to confirm the anointing on your life.

David was so anointed that Saul employed him in his army after he defeated Goliath with a sling and some rocks. He would eventually become

King of Israel and fulfill the prophetic words spoken over him by Samuel, but David had a little problem with lust.

DAVID'S LUST

We don't hear anything in scripture about David's problem with lust until 2 Samuel, chapter 11. Scripture says, "'When evening came, David got up from his bed and walked around on the roof of the royal palace. From the roof he saw a woman bathing, and she was very pretty. 3 David sent someone to ask about the woman. The man said, "She's Bathsheba, daughter of Eliam and wife of Uriah the Hittite." 4 So David sent messengers and took her. She came to him, and he went to bed with her. (She had just cleansed herself after her monthly period.) Then she went home'"

This is the first time we hear of David and his lust for women. However, David loved him some women—women from different cultures; black women, white women, Indian women, Asian, or Puerto Rican women—David was on it! He sleeps with another man's wife, gets her pregnant, and then has her husband killed—all to satisfy his lust. We often look past the fact that David always had women around. His first wife was named Michal. She was the daughter of King Saul. Saul gave her to David after he defeated the Philistines. David was also married to Ahinoam, Abigail, Haggith,

Abital, and eventually to Bathsheba. Each of his first six wives bore David a son. Bathsheba bore him four sons.

David knew Bathsheba did not belong to him. He knew that she was married, but lust wants what it wants, when it wants it. David said forget about the Kingdom, forget about my kids, forget about the anointing on my life, this woman is worth it. David is drawn away by his own lust. The book of James, chapter one, verse 14 teaches us that "Each person is tempted when they are dragged away by their own evil desire and enticed." Let's face it; when you want someone sexually, nobody has to force you to take your clothes off.

David did what he did willingly, and the worst part about his lust for Bathsheba is that David used his influence, his power, and his money—all of which came from God—to get what he wanted. Now we always talk about David's lust issues, but nobody forced Bathsheba to pull up at the palace either. She had a choice too, you know. Evidently, the spirit of lust was on her as well. The only thing two lustful people can produce is death. The bible says the wages of sin is death. His sin and her sin could only lead to destruction.

Single folk, stop saying someone is your mate and all you ever did was fornicate with them. The moment you slept with them you could potentially have destroyed any future you may have had together. If I could tell you about everyone I slept with before marriage...the ones I thought I would marry one day... Yeah, that worked out. Sin is sin and believers, in particular, know the consequences. How could an anointed King become so lustful that he would kill another woman's husband just to cover up his lust?

David's lust would eventually backfire on him. He gets Bathsheba pregnant and then has the nerve to think they she will have his baby. That's why he killed her husband, to cover up his lustful mistake. One thing you can never do is cover up your lust mistakes. Then David commits another sin; he has her husband murdered. When you cover up sin, you will continue to sin to cover up sin, perpetuating a cycle of sin and creating a mess out of which only God can get you. Scripture says that David realized his lust mistake and in 2 Samuel, verse12, David pleaded with God for the child's life. He fasted and spent the nights lying in sackcloth on the ground, but scripture says, "On the seventh day the child died. David's officials were afraid to tell him that the child was dead. They thought, While the child was alive, we talked to him, and he wouldn't listen to us. How can we tell him the child is dead? He may harm himself.

But when David saw that his officials were whispering to one another, he realized that the child was dead. "Is the child dead?" David asked them.

"Yes, he is dead," they answered.

So, David got up from the ground, bathed, anointed himself, and changed his clothes. He went into the Lord's house and worshiped. Then he went home and asked for food. They placed food in front of him, and he ate." David messed up but, at the end of the day, he was a worshiper. You may still deal with lust like David, but at the end of the day, you can go into worship and ask God to clean you out.

CHAPTER 3

LUST IN YOUR FAMILY

Newsflash! Yours is not the first family that has had to deal with the cycle of lust. David had children by his first wife Maacha—one named Tamar, and the other, Absalom. He also had another son by his wife Ahinoam. She bore him his son Amnon which made him the half-brother of Tamar and Absalom. Now keep in mind all of David's sons and daughters are living in the palace with David, who is the king. It is very hard to break the cycle of lust off your family when you have a lot of different spirits in your house—this mother's kids and that mother's kids and this brother who does not like that bother, and this sister who hates that sister.

But, before you judge David's house, take a moment and think about what's going on in your house. When you have a bunch of different spirits in your house something is bound to happen. Here we have an anointed king, chosen and anointed by God with a blended family and a bunch of different spirits. Yikes!

It is no wonder that some of our kids grow up confused sexually. Maybe you can trace it to all those different spirits they were around. David's life would eventually turn around, but lust remained in his family. I don't know about you, but I refuse to deal with the same demons that haunted my mother and my father. Some of us get comfortable with some of these demonic cycles, and we start saying stuff like, "Oh well, my dad did the same thing, and my mother did the same thing as well. I learned it from them, that's just how my parents were."

What! You have had several partners and you think that it's okay because that is what your parents did? That's a cycle with a spirit attached to it. You must break it. David never asked the Lord to break the cycle of lust off of his family. We can assume that he did not want the cycle of sin; of lust transferred to his kids, but he never took his problem to the Lord. As a result, in 2 Samuel 13, verses 4-14, we have one of the saddest stories of sexual abuse within a biblical family, and all because of a cycle of lust.

Tamar, Absalom, and Amnon are all around the same age. They have spent a considerable amount of time around each other. Can you imagine being the King's kids? If you can't, I need to talk to you, but that's another book! I can imagine what it would be like to be treated like royalty; having guards all around you; protective service, and servants around you all day, to meet your every need. You might get tired of being cooped up in the palace, with all these servants at your beck and call. I don't know if I would, but you might. Scripture says, "After this, David's son Amnon fell in love with Tamar, the beautiful sister of David's son Absalom. Amnon was so obsessed with his half-sister, Tamar, that he made himself sick. It seemed impossible for him to be alone with her because she was a virgin.

Amnon had a friend by the name of Jonadab, a son of David's brother Shimea. Jonadab was a very clever man. He asked Amnon, "Why are you, the king's son, so worn out morning after morning? Won't you tell me?"

"I'm in love with Absalom's sister, Tamar," he answered."

David's cycle of lust has now been transferred to his kids. His very own son is now in love with his sister.

IF YOU ARE GOING TO BREAK THE CYCLE OF LUST, YOU CAN'T LOVE WHAT YOU LUST AFTER.

Amnon is not lovesick, okay? He is lust sick! There are some people you think you are in love with, but it's really lust. If you don't believe me, just reflect back on how you all met. That will tell you everything about the nature and the direction of the relationship. Lust hides behind the word love. Most people get into lustful relationships because lust hides behind love. When someone lusts after you, they will tell you they love you to sleep with you. Once they sleep with you, they no longer love you. I remember when I was in the world; I used to use the love word to get what I wanted and then I was out. Amnon is lusting after Tamar and he is using the word love as bait, because he wants to get with her sexually.

THE BAIT OF LUST

Let's look closely at the cycle of lust. Remember, David inquired about Bathsheba from the rooftop of his palace. The bait he used was the power and status of being king. Once he attracted her with the bait to get her to come closer, it is very likely, at some point, that the word love came out his mouth. The next thing you know they are in bed together. To get in the relationships some of us are in right now, we used bait on someone, or someone used bait on us.

You saw he had a nice house and a nice car. He would occasionally let you stay there and drive the vehicle, but once he got a piece of your body, he cut you off and stop answering your calls. And, what about the woman on your job? She knows that you're married and you have children, but you look unhappy at work. She uses your distress to counsel you. The next thing you know you are in a six-month affair because she convinced you with her "fake" counseling that own wife is not good for you.

Bait, Bait, Bait. Lust will go out of its way to create something to lure you in. Hear me when I say this; lust is sneaky. It finds creative ways to mess up your life. Ammon communicates to me like a spoiled brat. I mean come on, he made himself sick. That is what spoiled people do. They create attention so people will feel sorry for them. That's exactly what Amnon did. He created a sickness to get attention. The crazy part is that he knew he would get it. He knew that faking illness would get him the attention he needed from Tamar. He took advantage of her caring heart, and used sickness as the bait. Do you know some people fall in love with the bait?

The money, the looks, the job, the position; Amnon probably said to himself, if Tamar falls for the bait, I got her. I want you to take a moment—those of you who have been tricked into some mess—and declare this over your life: "I will not fall for the bait another day in my life." Some of us got married to the wrong person because of the bait. Some of us had babies by people we now can't stand because we fell for the bait. Some of us even caught an STD because of the bait.

Some of us left churches because someone in the church used bait on you. Lust is not geographically restricted. It transcends cities, states, cultures, churches, and businesses. It wants what it wants.

BREAKING THE CYCLE OF LUST

YOU CAN'T SEXUALLY DESIRE PEOPLE IN

YOUR OWN FAMILY.

Amnon is so perverted that he is willing to take his own sister's virginity. Incest in the Bible refers "to sexual relations between certain close kinship relationships which are prohibited by the Hebrew bible. These prohibitions are found predominantly in Leviticus 18:8-18 and 20:11-21, but also in Deuteronomy. The biblical categories of prohibited relationships does not entirely match the modern definitions of prohibited relations in force in various countries or of the various Christian denominations."

A few books of the Bible, particularly the early parts of the Torah, contain narratives in which certain individuals, from the same family as one another, engage in sexual intercourse together; while this could be construed as incest, endogamy is an alternative interpretation. The Bible does not, for example, forbid cousins from marrying, but it does prohibit sexual relations with several other close relatives."

Amnon started sexually desiring his sister to the point that it turned into perversion. The definition of perversion is "the alteration of something from its original course, meaning, or state to a distortion or corruption of what was first intended." Another definition is "sexual behavior or desire that is considered abnormal or unacceptable." Amnon desiring his sister sexually is abnormal to the point he is willing to hurt her and others to have her.

Let me tell you what else is abnormal sexual behavior; staying on that computer or that phone until 2 or 3 in the morning looking at explicitly lustful pictures and videos. You would be amazed at how many of the saints in key positions within the church indulge in this private perversion. A few years ago, I went to a church conference with hundreds of people in attendance. I was late for a particular session I wanted to attend and asked an employee were this particular room was and they showed me. As they walk me to the room, he asked if I was a pastor. I said yes, and he went on to tell me "I know you guys are churchgoers, but our pay-per-view sales skyrocket because of all the pornographic movies ordered whenever we hold this conference here."

I was like are you sure it's when this conference is going on, and he said, "I have been employed here for years. I am positive." I had to ask myself, I wonder how many of these believers came to this conference to indulge in some of their lustful behaviors? I was embarrassed, because although the man had not said it, I am sure he probably considered me to be just like them. I went on to say, "Man. I am sorry to hear that. However, some of us have control and actually live holy lives."

I immediately began thinking about the many generations of lust—cycles of lust at the conference that had not been broken. One thing is for sure; a lustful person will find another lustful person, quick. It's like you can sense when someone wants the same thing that you want. I know David had a heart for God. However, I also know that David, knowingly or unknowingly, passed the cycle of lust down to his children and his children's children.

There are some things you may be facing in regards to lust, that did not start with you. In fact, you very well may be living with a demon your grandmother or your grandfather never cast out; a curse they never broke. As a result, your house may be divided. Your kids may be disobedient and engaged in all kinds of ungodly behaviors, all because you may be living with a transgenerational cycle of lust.

CHAPTER 4

LUSTFUL PEOPLE HANG AROUND LUSFUL PEOPLE

2 Samuel 13 verse 5 says, "'Go to bed and pretend to be ill," Jonadab said. "When your father comes to see you, say to him, 'I would like my sister Tamar to come and give me something to eat. Let her prepare the food in my sight so I may watch her and then eat it from her hand.'" Amnon had people in his life that struggled with the same thing he did. The worst part about all this is the advice Jonadab gave him is what drove him to take this vicious act.

IF YOU ARE GOING TO BREAK THE CYCLE OF LUST YOU CAN'T HANG OUT WITH OR GET ADVICE FROM PEOPLE WHO HAVE THE SAME CYCLE OF LUST AS YOU.

Jonadab had the same struggle. How do you figure that Pastor? Because anyone that can devise a plan for you to intentionally hurt someone else is wrong. The advice that Jonadab gave him was something he was probably thinking about for himself.

The older saints use to say it real deep and prophetic like this, "Birds of a feather flock together." Stop declaring that God has delivered you from sexual sin, but hanging around people who have the same struggle. If you are struggling with lust, I would be very careful about who you hang around with. I would not advise you to keep company or to travel with others who have the same issues. Something is bound to happen.

There are many Pastors, business people, CEO's, etc., who travel with people who have similar issues of the flesh. Then they have the nerve to think they are slick, like nobody knows what's going on. I know what's going on. They are attempting to cover up their lustful behavior, with someone who has the same struggle. I am not only a pastor, but I am also a business owner. I have owned a barbershop for almost eleven years now.

Younger barbers, coming out of barber school, constantly ask me if they can serve as an apprentice under me. Whenever I hear those words, my spiritual ears hear "mentorship." I have had a few apprentices in my shop and I literally have to teach them barber shop etiquette; cuts of all types including low even temp fades, bald fades, texturizers, hair dyes, and razor work. It's almost like they are in school again. I spend hours re-teaching them, because working in an actual shop and being in barber school are two different things.

Before they can cut on the floor on a weekly basis, I make sure they are professional and well trained. As a Pastor, I see this approach to mentorship in ministry done wrong. I see some leaders hanging around people who they find attractive and working close to them, even traveling on the road with them supposedly so they can mentor them.

You do know that some of this is not mentorship. If we both have the same struggle, we can hide our struggle with each other on the road. So, if I tell people I am mentoring you, and I am an influential leader, people naturally will believe it. Listen to me when I tell you, God is bringing judgment on those who engage in such behavior. God is no longer allowing leaders to get away with the word "mentorship" when they are really trying to cover up sin.

You would be amazed at the number of influential people who have been getting away with this for years. I came to announce to you that this day is over. God is raising a new generation of leaders who have standards and morals, and who conduct themselves with integrity. For the undiscovered leader listening; the one who is anointed by God and gifted by God—your time is coming soon!

God sees your heart and your sacrifice. The worst thing to witness is a leader who influences thousands of people, but has no control over his flesh. Let me say this to those leaders—who may be convicted. God did not send you to those people for you to sleep with them. He sent them to you for you to cover them through their issues, not so you can pretend to help them and take advantage of them.

(GET CONTROL OVER YOURSELF).

Years ago, when we had a very prominent leader fall from grace, we spoke so negatively of him. What bothers me is that most of the men and women who crucified this leader may never have prayed for him, or even asked God to restore him. The church has become so obsessed with scandal and the minutiae of ministry, that we forget why God called us, which was to bring healing and comfort to the lost and broken.

LUST LOVES TO STARE

The b clause of verse 5 says "Let her prepare the food in my sight so I may watch her and then eat it from her hand." Notice closely in the text that Jonadab gave him more bad counsel by insisting that Tamar prepare food in Amnon's sight. (FLESH IS WATCHING) then he says so I may watch her (FLESH IS WATCHING) and then eat it from her hand. (FLESH WANTS TO TOUCH). If your flesh stares at something it wants for a long time, actions will soon follow.

Guarding the eye gate is so important when talking about fleshly desires. See Jonadab and Amnon came up with a plan based on what they saw. I am sure that Tamar was gorgeous and had everything a man would desire, however sometimes beauty can become a curse. They stared at her day after day and allowed her beauty to controlled their appetites and sexual desires. They went from staring to imaging. What do you do when looks lead into someone's bedroom? It's no secret that porn has become mainstream entertainment in our society.

From popular porn sites putting up billboards in New York City's Times Square to online news sources like Buzz Feed normalizing porn with viral videos, it feels like porn is everywhere you look. Porn is plastered all over social media sites like Facebook and Instagram. It's too easy to see on Twitter, especially considering that the "Twitterverse" is home to an estimated 10+ million porn accounts. Pornography is an estimated $97 billion dollar business. According to science and research, thousands of people, including porn performers themselves, confirm that porn has seriously damaged their lives and their relationships.

According to a 2004 study in Social Science Quarterly, people who admit to having extramarital affairs were over 300% more likely to admit consuming porn than those who have never had an affair. At least 30% of all data transferred across the internet is porn-related. The devil knows that if he can just get you to see something you want, he can destroy your life. That's the power that lust can have over your life. Just think if you never looked at any explicitly sexual images, if you had not stared and allowed your imagination to start wandering, you would not be in the situation you're in now. Lust is a real devil and it is looking to tear your family, your business, your career, your church, and your finances apart. Lust tears everything apart.

Even Job struggled with lust because he said in Job 31:1 "I made a covenant with my eyes not to look lustfully at a girl." What must Job have seen to make a covenant with his eyes? It is significant that in this long section where Job explained his righteous life, he began by noting that he guarded himself from looking lustfully upon young women. This rightly suggests that a man's ability to not look upon lustful images is an important indicator of his general righteousness and blamelessness.

I believe righteousness is tied to that at which you decide to look. This also suggests that the eyes are a gateway for lust, especially for men. This is demonstrated over and over again by both personal experience and empirical study. When a man places enticing, sensual, lust-inducing images before his eyes, it is a form of foreplay, especially considering that it often or frequently causes some level of sexual arousal in the man.

In Hebrews, the same word signifies both an eye and a fountain; to show, said one, that from the eye, as a fountain, flows both sin and misery."

When Job says that he has made a covenant with his eyes to abstain from lust, he does not mean that he has stopped experiencing lust altogether. What he means is that he refuses to dwell upon the lustful feelings which, as the normal red-blooded male he is, come to him very naturally. Job insisted that he would not look upon a young woman - a maiden in this way.

This was especially meaningful, because in that culture it would be somewhat accepted for a rich and powerful man like Job to seduce or ravish a maiden, and then add her as either a wife or a concubine. Job restrained himself from women that others in his same circumstances would not restrain themselves from.

Job exemplified what true deliverance is by restraining his eyes from looking at something he knows he could have. Because in our society, we are bombarded with sexual images, we have to make constant decisions regarding the images at which we gaze. (TAKE A SECOND AND MAKE A COVENANT WITH YOUR EYES, AND SAY LORD HELP ME TO SEE WHAT YOU SEE).

Amnon had been staring at his sister for months and after a while, he made up in his mind that he was going to get her. Different things about you, attract different people. When I first got into ministry, I thought folks were attracted to me because I was young or because I had on a nice shirt or suit.

The Lord corrected my flesh one day, saying "It's neither. It is the anointing I have placed on your life." The challenge, when you have a lust issue, is that you will think that people who are drawn to you are people who want to sleep with you. Sorry to burst your bubble, but those people are drawn to you because of your anointing. Your anointing carries a fragrance, wherever you go.

If you notice in 2 Samuel verse 2, Amnon mentioned that he was in love with Tamar, his brother Absalom's sister. Amnon did not allow himself to call Tamar his sister – instead, she was Absalom's sister. The power of lust is strong enough to twist the way we see reality. Lust loves to stare, especially at what isn't there. Interestingly enough, whatever lust says it is, becomes your reality.

Amon is trying to justify his lustful ways by telling himself that it's okay to look and lust over her. So, he creates this fake reality in his head— probably saying to himself, "It's ok, man, you guys have different mothers, and she may not be fully related." You know what lust does. You see a cousin that's attractive and lust takes over and says, "Well we don't know each other. We just met." What! You are lying to yourself to justify your self-gratification. Lust is a monster. Rather than to disconnect himself from his lust issue, he disconnects himself from his reality. He lets lust lead him into denial—denying the fact that she was his sister.

Lust only sees fairy tales, saying stuff to you like, "Cheat on your wife. Be with her on the side and live happily ever after. Cheat on your husband and then leave him. You too will have a happy life. Sleep with your best friend's girlfriend or boyfriend. No one will ever know.

The lustful pastor says to himself, "he or she is looking at me. Maybe I can give them an assignment just to get close to them. No one will know." Or how about the CEO of a company who misappropriates funds to take his side piece on vacation? Or what about the sexual predator that has a secret crush on little boys, or little girls? Lust tells them nothing is wrong with you—what you desire is natural.

Lust only sees fairy tales. Lust is a Monster looking to devour your life. The devil is masterful at influencing. He understands that the way to your head is through your eye gate. As masterful as the enemy is at influencing through the eye gate, God knows and sees all. For a long time, the church has been silent regarding sexual issues that consistently come up in our churches, amongst our families.

For years we have been silent, we have not said anything about the men and women of God that have been involved in sexual cases regarding minors. We have swept these issues under the rug and continued to have church as normal. What! We, as leaders, are to be held accountable for our actions. My home church, the church I grew up in was Gospel Temple Church of God in Christ (COGIC) in Saint Paul, Minnesota. My great uncle, who has gone on to be with Jesus, started the church over some 60 years ago. After he died, my grandmother pastored the church for many years, and now my father, Pastor Dwight Buckner, Sr., is pastor. When I was a child, people would have to sit down because of their lustful behavior. If you had a child out of wedlock, and you sang in the choir, you had to sit until you realized what you did. If you played the drums, keyboard, bass, or whatever, and the Pastor found out that you were openly sinning, you took a seat.

This was not to embarrass you, but to restore you. When did we get to a place in the church where we can sin one day, and stand in the pulpit the next day? Leaders are not being completely restored, and the congregants will do what the leader does; unfortunately, sometimes in access. Talking to leaders who have it all together, it is not cool to lead a bunch of people who live in any kind of way.

Not under my leadership! You can call me young and old school if you want, but wrong is wrong and sin is still sin. The church has allowed spiritual gifts to be more important than living a holy lifestyle. If they can sing, play, or preach, we look the other way about their outside lifestyle. For years I questioned why God had me in the backwoods for so long. I spent a lot of days angry and upset because I saw people preaching all across the country with huge churches that I knew personally did not live holy lives. One day, I said, "Lord, what am I doing wrong?" God spoke through time and said, "Nothing. I am protecting you and your name from all of the corruption I see in the church. Your time will come, and when it does you will speak change over thousands of lives. "

From that day forward I said, Lord, let every one of my sermons bring change and not hype. I want to preach to people until tears fall and conviction runs all over them. Take a moment after reading this chapter and ask God to send people into your life to hold you accountable.

CHAPTER 5

LUST   IS   ONLY   IN   CERTAIN   ROOMS

Ok! Let me just say this upfront. You do not belong in every room with everybody. Nor do you need to be up close to everyone. The wrong room can be a trap and mess up your whole life. Scripture says in 2 Samuel 13:7, "David sent word to Tamar at the palace: "Go to the house of your brother Amnon and prepare some food for him." So Tamar went to the house of her brother Amnon, who was lying down. She took some dough, kneaded it, made the bread in his sight and baked it. Then she took the pan and served him the bread, but he refused to eat.

"Send everyone out of here," Amnon said. So everyone left him. Then Amnon said to Tamar, "Bring the food here into my bedroom so I may eat from your hand." Amnon's behavior was childish, and David indulged him. Amnon acted like a baby. It is childish to refuse food because it is not served the way we want it. From this and other passages, it appears that David was generally indulgent towards his children. This may be because he felt guilty for having so many wives, children, and responsibilities as the king. He didn't have or didn't take the time to be a true father to his children. He dealt with the guilt by being soft and overindulgent with his children.

Amnon took Jonadab's wicked advice quickly and completely. It's too bad that men don't often respond to godly advice the same way. (IF

YOU'RE GOING TO BREAK THE CYCLE OF LUST YOU CAN ONLY GO INTO CERTAIN ROOM)

Tamar had no clue that this room represented a trap for her. She went in with good intentions, she went in because he was her blood brother. Let me say this. It's hard to predict some people's motives because they come across as cool, nice, friendly, and polite. The crazy part about some people, including family, is that some folk just want you to get caught up in their mess.

Genesis 39 gives us another great example of the importance of staying out of certain rooms. The bible says that "'Joseph was well-built and handsome, and after a while his master's wife took notice of Joseph and said, "Come to bed with me!" But he refused. "With me in charge," he told her, "my master does not concern himself with anything in the house; everything he owns he has entrusted to my care. No one is greater in this house than I am. My master has withheld nothing from me except you, because you are his wife. How then could I do such a wicked thing and sin against God?" And though she spoke to Joseph day after day, he refused to go to bed with her or even be with her.'"

I know we talk about God anointing our "Yes's,' but this season God said he is going to anoint your "No." You will have to be like Joseph and have a divine refusal in you. If someone tries to tempts you to do the wrong thing, or if you temp someone to do the wrong thing, you need to tell yourself "No way." The reality is that some things are not worth your destiny, Beloved.

One day Joseph, "went into the house to attend to his duties, and none of the household servants was inside. She caught him by his cloak and said, "Come to bed with me!" But he left his cloak in her hand and ran out of the house.

Notice that she waited until there were just the two of them in the room. She cared nothing about his position, his name, or anything else. She just wanted his body. She lusted after him. Listen, I am trying to prevent you from doing something you will regret in the future. She did not care about her reputation because she knew she could cover her mess since Joseph had somewhat of a shady past. Some people invite you into rooms so they can mess you up and cover their tracks. I believe God used Joseph to reveal to Potiphar that his wife was a little sneaky. A man generally knows his wife and a woman knows her husband.

This is not in the text, but let me use a little eisegesis. Let's explore. I think that one of the reasons that Potiphar sent Joseph to prison was to prevent himself from looking like a fool. Rather than to declare that Joseph was innocent, he declared him guilty—to save his reputation and to salvage his pride.

"'When she saw that he had left his cloak in her hand and had run out of the house, she called her household servants. "Look," she said to them, "this Hebrew has been brought to us to make sport of us! He came in here to sleep with me, but I screamed. When he heard me scream for help, he left his cloak beside me and ran out of the house."

She kept his cloak beside her until his master came home. Then she told him this story: "That Hebrew slave you brought us came to me to make sport of me. But as soon as I screamed for help, he left his cloak beside me and ran out of the house."'

She trapped Joseph in a room full of lies and lust, and, more importantly, in her mess. Truth is, she was lustful, not Joseph. She blamed her lust on him, so she could look righteous. No matter how much you cover up your lust with lies, in the end, whatever you tried to create in that room will be revealed. There are sexual addicts out there who need help—people like Potiphar's wife, but she blamed her addiction on Joseph. I bet you a lot of the servants in that house ended up in jail over her addiction and her lies, all because she refused to get help.

WHO IS SENDING THE INVITATION?

When you are invited into certain rooms with "quote unquote" important people, check the reputation of the person sending the invitation. Up to this point in the story, Amnon had an okay reputation, but remember he still has the cycle of lust in him from his father David. They all lived in the same house and they all knew about Daddy's struggle. They also knew that Daddy had gotten older, but he had never dealt with his lust issue. If you don't deal with your lust it's not going anywhere.

You can clean your computer off, you can throw the condoms out, you can take medication for the S.T.D., and you can stop dating a bunch of people. However, if you have not specifically and deliberately asked God to deliver you, the lust demon is still in you, and you will not find out until the devil sends something or someone to trigger it. Every invitation should not be accepted.

Stop thinking because people come from good families or have good jobs, or are prominent in the church, that their invitations are God sent. Let's look at this invitation Amnon sent Tamar. He told his father to have her send him some food because he was sick. Lustful people will send other people to get you. If you remember his father, David, did the same thing with Bathsheba. Trust me when I tell you that the devil knows how to send nice invitations.

I remember attending a former church's anniversary years ago. The pastor knew me, however, he did not know a few of the people I had with me. He sent one of his armor bearers to get me, so that he could meet a particular person who was with me. His motives were all wrong and the person I was with knew this too.

This was a friend I'd known for years, and he used me to get to someone else. How do I know that? Because lustful invitations will always lead you to a lustful room by yourself. Amnon's invitation was to lead Tamar to one place, his room. The connection that I am trying to make is lust needs a room in which to function. Why didn't Amnon invite her into the kitchen, or the front yard, or even the patio? His goal was to assault her behind closed doors where no one could see him.

LUST HAS A PRIVATE REPUTATION

Amnon kept this a secret with Jonadab because he was trying to protect what little reputation he had. He still had thoughts of having the kingdom one day. He understood that if he was going to yield to the lust demon passed down from his father, he had to do it privately.

Years ago, when I first started serving in

ministry again, I submitted to God. I started serving in my local church, I attended bible college and eventually seminary. When I completely understood that I would be in ministry for the rest of my life, I figured I would serve in youth ministry first and then start pastoring a few months later. Little did I know that God was taking me the long route (and He still is) in order to work out my private reputation.

I still struggled with lust while serving in ministry. You can't fool God with your private reputation. There is a you that everybody knows, then there is a you that only you and God know. I will admit that there were endless lustful relationships that I stayed in because I did not want to be lonely. You know how some of us will get into relationships with people because we hate the thought of being by ourselves. I remember dating someone and falling into a life of fornication. Then I went to a bible study one night and God convicted me because of my private life. Can I tell you that your private life is not private? I had to ask God to change me so that he could completely use me.

I don't know about you, but whenever I deliberately disobey God, He strips me down until I realize that it is only by his grace and mercy that I have made it this far. Some of you reading this book have gotten caught up in a cycle of private lust. Your reputation is great in public, but in private it's horrible. Pastor how did I get into this private cycle of lust? I am glad you asked. You got into it by lying to yourself; thinking you are someone or somewhere you are not. Some of you have lost your families, your finances, and almost your faith and you still will not listen or should I say, "Harken unto the voice of the Lord."

What is it going to take for you to break this cycle of lust? Lustful people love to be surrounded by people who baby them. Amnon was acting like a child. He cried until he got what he wanted. If you are reading this and you do this, stop acting like a baby! You are getting too old to be making the same mistakes. I guess you will not be happy until God closes all the doors He has opened for you. You even think God is going to baby you; saying stuff like, Lord, I promise I will not do it again—in your baby voice. He delivers you and you do it again and again.

I made myself a promise last year. I am not going to contribute to anyone else's dysfunction. In Deuteronomy 2, scripture says, "'then we turned back and set out toward the wilderness along the route to the Red Sea, as the Lord had directed me. For a long time, we made our way around the hill country of Seir. Then the Lord said to me, "You have made your way around this hill country long enough; now turn north."'"

The cycle of lust is a mountain that many of us continue to go around because we are hard-headed. God had to eventually speak to Moses to tell them to turn north. In other words, try a new route. Try some new friends. Try living right and try God. Whatever you do stop, taking chances. Your public reputation should match your private reputation. Amnon's true character emerged when Tamar realized his real intent. This was something she was not expecting. In the 11th verse of this chapter, it states, "But when she took it to him to eat, he grabbed her and said, "Come to bed with me, my sister."

LUST ALWAYS HAS A MOTIVE

Ammon's motives were revealed. Tamar was in shock and could not believe that her brother wanted to sleep with her. She was afraid, shocked and scared, and at that moment, she had no escape. What do you do when you find out that the people closest to you; the people that you love, have the wrong motives towards you? Amnon's evil naturally revealed itself. Here, he admitted his incestuous desire as he made the wicked suggestion to Tamar. Amnon seemed to be a spoiled prince who always took what he wanted. He revealed to Tamar that he wanted to sleep with her. Be warned Beloved—people will use several ways to get you in the bed. In my journey with God, He has revealed people's motives and let me know why they get close to me.

Amnon was not just Tamar's half-brother he was also influential to Tamar. What do you do when you find out influential people have the wrong motive for getting close to you? Some people like Amnon, who are influential, will test you just to see how far you will go. Amnon knew he had influence over Tamar because he was older and in line to gain the kingdom. Some people will take advantage of you because they feel you need them more than they need you.

Amnon knew that if he told Tamar to come to his room, she would give him what he wanted because of who he was. If you are in leadership and you have been taking advantage of innocent people, trying to feed your lust using your God-given influence, please know that God will deal with you.

God will strip you of your influence and embarrass you. I have seen churches fall to pieces because of lustful leaders who lace their issue in lust. Lust is a user. It uses whoever it pleases to accomplish what it set out to do. However, lust will always live a trail. "No, my brother!" she said to him. "Don't force me! Such a thing should not be done in Israel! Don't do this wicked thing. Lust will always force itself on you like Amnon forced himself on his sister. How many times have you forced yourself on people with your lustful habits?

When I was in the world, I was extremely

lustful. I remember dating one person for a while and we broke up. My cycle of lust was so bad that I did not care if she fell in love with someone else, I just did not want her to have sex with anybody else. Crazy, right? Lust makes you think you own people. Amnon was likely thinking that he owned Tamar in his room. Get out of rooms where people think they own you. Tamer did not give herself away to Amnon. What makes matters worse is the fact that she was a virgin. Her virginity was stolen by a lustful person.

Lust will steal your innocence. It will contaminate what God meant to be pure and holy. Sex within the context of marriage, between a man and a woman, is beautiful, but when lust takes over, it follows no rules, respects no boundaries, and turns what is meant to be pure into something evil. A part of me wishes that Tamar had never gone into her brother's room. However, lust vacations in privacy.

CHAPTER SIX

LUST   DOES   NOT   CARE   WHO   IT   HURTS

Tamar responds in 2 Samuel 13, saying, "'What about me? Where could I get rid of my disgrace? And what about you? You would be like one of the wicked fools in Israel. Please speak to the king; he will not keep me from being married to you.' But he refused to listen to her, and since he was stronger than she, he raped her.'"

The real question is, how many people have you hurt? When I was in the world, all I could think about was getting mine. It was not until years later after I got saved and active in ministry that God convicted me about all the people I had taken advantage of with my lust. Truth is, every person with whom we may have done something lustful were not all bad people. Have you ever considered the fact that your lust may have messed up what God intended to be a good relationship?

Lust will almost always hurt innocent people. When you indulge in your lust, you hurt yourself, you hurt your family, and you hurt everyone connected to you. Amnon was more than forceful, he was a monster. Tamar could easily see how evil and disgraceful this was. Amnon could not see what was so plainly evident because he was blinded by lust. Tamar wisely asks Amnon to consider the result of his desire, both for her and for him. In Tamar's tender speech, she asked Amnon to consider what he was getting himself into and was it worth it? That's the question I want to pose to you. Have you considered how many people you will hurt if you continue in this cycle of lust? God gave Amnon more than enough time to correct his mistakes.

LUST WILL NOT LET YOU CORRECT YOUR

MISTAKES

Just think about how long Amnon thought about committing this act. He was so caught up in his lust that he went too far to let it go. Tamar even knew that lust was not his normal behavior, but the spirit and the cycle of lust began to overtake him—the cycle of lust from his father and his grandfather. The bible never mentions David's father, Jesse, as being lustful it just identifies him as David's father. David, however, had to get this cycle of lust from somewhere. What Amnon was facing was deeper than just a lust moment.

He was dealing with a transgenerational demon. When Tamar pleaded with him to consider, he took her body by force. Anything that can completely take over and control your body and make you do something so evil is a demon. Demons understand the gift of free will. After all, each demon knows that he deliberately and willfully chose to rebel against God. Therefore, their greatest delight occurs when they can lead young people to make foolish choices. Demons know that these choices and the subsequent actions can produce unbearable misery for a lifetime. The demons carefully study each of us from birth to determine how the inescapable consequences of sin can be used to ruin us.

Whenever there is a great call on a family, there are also great demons to face. David's lineage was chockfull of tormenting, lustful demons. Even David's wisest son, Solomon, struggled with lust demons for scripture says in 1 kings 11, that "Solomon loved many foreign women. Besides the daughter of the king of Egypt he married Hittite women and women from Moab, Ammon, Edom, and Sidon. He married them even though the Lord had commanded the Israelites not to intermarry with these people, because they would cause the Israelites to give their loyalty to other gods. Solomon married seven hundred princesses and also had three hundred concubines. They made him turn away from God."

Solomon faced the same cycle of lust. This cycle made Solomon turn against God. How could a man with such wisdom make such foolish decisions? Easy answer; he didn't, his lust did. Lust will make all kinds of disastrous decisions for you if you let it. Ask yourself how you ended up having children with men you hate or a woman you can't stand. How could I have stepped out on my wife or husband multiple times? How did I have this many sexual partners in one year? Lust will not let you correct your mistakes.

Oftentimes, after we have allowed our flesh to control us, it's too late to go back and fix our mistakes. Scripture says that by the time that Solomon, "was old they had led him into the worship of foreign gods. He was not faithful to the Lord his God, as his father David had been." Solomon's flesh had him worshiping other Gods. Whatever flesh worships, you will worship.

IF YOU DON'T BREAK THE CYCLE OF LUST, IT WILL AFFECT YOUR WORSHIP

Solomon stopped worshiping the God of his father, David, and started worshiping the God of the lustful woman he was with. I remember falling in sexual sin years ago with a woman who was also in the church. This was way, way before I was married, of course. I remember going to bible study a few days after we fell in sin, and my worship was in a completely different place. I was supposed to be there to worship the King of Kings, but all I could do was replay the lustful encounter. Before I knew it, my mind was gone and after bible study, I went right back over there.

The cycle of lust had completely stolen my worship. This woman then became my idol and my God, because all I could do was think about her. Anything and anybody that can get that much attention from you, can become an idol. Eventually, you will worship that person or that thing. Lust will take you into unfamiliar places and give you a mindset you have never had. Scripture says, "Even though the Lord, the God of Israel, had appeared to Solomon twice and had commanded him not to worship foreign gods, Solomon did not obey the Lord but turned away from him. So the Lord was angry with Solomon and said to him, "Because you have deliberately broken your covenant with me and disobeyed my commands, I promise that I will take the kingdom away from you and give it to one of your officials.'"

Solomon's heart and his worship was no longer with God, but with the gods of other women. For that reason, God stripped him of the kingdom. Some of you reading this need to understand that you have too much to lose because you cannot control your flesh. Do you care about your future enough to resist the enemy you see today?

LUST IS ABUSIVE

The outcome of Amnon's lust was harmful, shameful, and irrevocable. This is what happens when your lust is out of control. You hurt innocent people. In the scripture, Tamar says, "How could I ever hold up my head in public again? And you—you would be completely disgraced in Israel. Please, speak to the king, and I'm sure that he will give me to you." The Law of Moses commanded against any marriage between a half-brother and half-sister. Tamar probably said this simply as a ploy to get away from Amnon.

If you don't break the cycle, lust will take advantage of innocent people. Amnon is willing to take whatever he wanted, and he shows by his actions that he could have cared less about her disgrace. Scripture says, "But he would not listen to her; and since he was stronger than she was, he overpowered her and raped her."

I want to take a moment and apologize to everyone whose innocence was stolen because of sexual abuse. I want to tell you that I am sorry that you had to go through that. Not only did Ammon rape his sister, Tamar, but he stole her virginity. She had to live the rest of her life with the abuse in her head. Over and over again she had to replay the image of her brother raping her because of the cycle of lust. David's failure to break the cycle resulted in the transfer of the same negative cycle of abuse to his children and possibly his children's children and so on—potentially for generations.

One in five women and one in 71 men will be raped at some point in their lives. In the U.S., one in three women and one in six men experienced some form of contact sexual violence in their lifetime. 51.1% of female victims of rape reported being raped by an intimate partner and 40.8% by an acquaintance, and 52.4% of male victims report being raped by an acquaintance and 15.1% by strangers. Almost half (49.5%) of multiracial women and over 45% of American Indian/Alaska Native women were subjected to some form of contact sexual violence in their lifetime. 91% of victims of rape and sexual assault are female, and nine percent are male. In eight out of 10 cases of rape, the victim knew the perpetrator.

If you have been abused, I want you to know that you did not deserve it. You did not do or say anything to bring this on yourself, but it had everything to do with the cycle of lust still alive in the person that hurt you. God will have the last say for what they did. Tamar had to spend the rest of her life with guilt and shame caused by someone else's lust. There are a lot of Tamar's out there who have been victims of someone else's lust.

Recently, I have seen a number of young boys that have been abused by men, and this is in the church. I have consoled young men who have been sexually abused by someone they looked up to and admired. I could not tell you how it has ripped apart their lives and careers because they continue to replay the sad memories of someone's lust overtaking and stealing from them. The sad part about this text is most read it and hear Tamar's name and associate her immediately with rape.

Lust is abusive. Sometimes, I ask God how can something like this go on so often—rape, sex trafficking, molestation, etc.—why is it so prevalent in our society?

Scripture tells us, "'Then Amnon was filled with a deep hatred for her; he hated her now even more than he had loved her before. He said to her, "Get out!"'

"No," she answered. "To send me away like this is a greater crime than what you just did!"

But Amnon would not listen to her; he called in his personal servant and said, "Get this woman out of my sight! Throw her out and lock the door!"'

This revealed Amnon's attraction for Tamar for what it was – lust, not love. Amnon was attracted to Tamar for what he could get from her, not out of concern for her. In many lustful relationships, there is a combination of both love and lust, but in Amnon's attraction, there was only lust. In his single-minded lust, Amnon only built upon the example of his father David. David was never this dominated by lust, but he was pointed in the same direction. David's multiple marriages and his adultery with Bathsheba displayed this same direction. This is often how "the iniquity of the fathers is carried on by the children to the third and fourth generations."

A child will often model a parent's sinful behavior; sometimes going further in the direction of sin the parent is pointed towards. Amnon had no real love for Tamar, only lust – and so he immediately felt guilty over his sin. Tamar was simply a reminder of his foolish sin. He wanted every reminder of his sin to be put far away.

Ammon immediately looked at Tamar with disgust. God was reminding him of his sin, and the aftereffect of his sin. Most lustful people will be faced with the reality of what they did. Amnon, unwilling to deal with his crime, blamed his lust cycle on Tamer and hated her. Hold on how are you mad at somebody of whom you took advantage? Lustful people who take advantage of others, are rarely able to look you in the face and admit they were wrong.

One of my favorite movies is a movie called *Antwon Fisher*. In this film, we meet a young man named Antwon played by Derek Luke. He is beaten as a child, yelled at, and even sexually abused by members of his foster family—those who were entrusted to care for him. When he got older, he decided to go to the navy, but his sexual abuse and the torture he had experienced as a child kept eating away at him. He would have moments where he would lose it and start fighting. Because he was carrying the anger from what happened to him as a child, he was easily agitated. Eventually, after being in the navy for a while, he built up enough faith and courage to go find his real mother and father. He is also lead to go by his former abusers' house. They answer the door and try to greet him with a hug, but Antwon pushes them away. He looks them in the eyes, and says, You tried to hurt me, but I am still standing."

His abusers never look him in the eye, they cannot because they are faced with the reality of what they did to him as a defenseless child. Lust is an abuser. When the time comes for you to face the one who abused you sexually because of their unresolved lust issues, trust me, if they are not already dead or in jail, they will come face-to-face with the reality of their bad decisions. You know you reap what you sow.

This cycle of lust that you might be dealing with can lead you to a path down which you never thought you would go. That's why it's so important that you begin to ask God to help you break this cycle. The iniquity of the fathers is carried on by the children to the third and fourth generations. Beloved, this is a cycle. You might not understand where you are in the cycle, but you can make a decision not to carry this on to the next generation.

Break the cycle! Ask God to give you the strength to get out of whatever trap, whatever dark place you are in and to set you free from years of bondage. Your mother and father may not have known to break the cycle, but you still have time to act now. Take a second even now and ask God to help you break the curse. Ask him to break the negative cycle off your life, not only so you can be free, but so your children and your children's children can be free as well.

This is so important, and just in case you still don't understand the significance, let me leave you with one more thing. We have talked about David's problem with lust and how his failure to address the issue had disastrous results, but if we were to go a bit deeper, we would have to talk about David's son Absalom. You see Absalom was angry about what Amnon did to Tamar and he could not understand why David did not punish Amnon. This triggered other negative family dynamics: anger, dysfunction, jealousy, violence, competition, and more. Perhaps this is the subject of another book, but I implore you, Beloved, break the cycle of lust today!

Scripture References are from the New International Version (NIV)

Statistics regarding pornography – Yahoo Finance

Sexual assault statistics- National Sexual Violence Resource Center (NSVRC)

www.ingramcontent.com/pod-product-compliance
Lightning Source LLC
Chambersburg PA
CBHW061045050726
47592CB00004B/1594